Warren Dotz

Masud Husain

dog food for thought

Pet Food Label Art, Wit & Wisdom

INSIGHT EDITIONS

San Rafael, California

PO Box 3088
San Rafael, CA 94912
www.insighteditions.com

Copyright © 2014 Warren Dotz

All rights reserved. No part of this book may be reproduced in any form without written permission from the publisher.

Library of Congress Cataloging-in-Publication Data available.

ISBN: 978-1-60887-358-6

Book concept: Warren Dotz • Masud Husain
Cover and book design: Masud Husain

Visit the authors at: warrendotz.com • masudhusain.com

Find us on Facebook: www.facebook.com/InsightEditions
Follow us on Twitter: @insighteditions

ROOTS of PEACE   REPLANTED PAPER

Insight Editions, in association with Roots of Peace, will plant two trees for each tree used in the manufacturing of this book. Roots of Peace is an internationally renowned humanitarian organization dedicated to eradicating land mines worldwide and converting war-torn lands into productive farms and wildlife habitats. Roots of Peace will plant two million fruit and nut trees in Afghanistan and provide farmers there with the skills and support necessary for sustainable land use.

Manufactured in China by Insight Editions

10 9 8 7 6 5 4 3 2 1

PET'S NAME

Dog lovers
have always delighted in feeding and caring for their
pets. These pages—through their pairing of rare and quirky
images and select verse—evoke that joy, and then some.

The period extending from the early 1950s through the late
'70s was not only the apex of independently owned pet
food companies and supermarkets, it was also a time when
the creative flourish of modern aesthetics was incorporated
into label design. And so, many of the pet food labels and
boxes showcased here are among the best and boldest that
commercial advertising had to offer.

Look closely and you will see that graphic design was
increasingly influenced by comic book and television
cartoon illustration, children's breakfast cereal branding, and
breakthroughs in contemporary typography and printing.

This wonderful commercial artwork, coupled with quotations
about the lovable attributes of canines, is truly
food for thought.

ASTRO
Astro Pet Foods and Supplies
Brightwaters, New York

You can run with the big dogs
or sit on the porch and bark.

COWBOY WISDOM

ASTRO

for dogs

NET WT. 14½ OZ.

CHUNKS Beef
meat by-products

"Pedigree Products to Please Your Pet"

I love dogs.

They live in the moment and don't care
about anything except affection and food.

DAVID DUCHOVNY

ACTOR

NET WT. 15½ OZ.

BINGOS
American Pet Food Company
Yakima, Washington

There was a farmer who had a dog,
And Bingo was his name-o.
B-I-N-G-O

CHILDREN'S FOLK SONG LYRIC

BONNIE
Bonnie Dog Food Company
Sacramento, California

When a dog food is "new and improved," who tests it?

ANON.

My dog, she looks at me sometimes with that look, and I think maybe deep down inside she must know exactly how I feel. But then maybe she just wants the food off my plate.

ANON.

BONUS

NET WT.
15½ OZS.

Dog
FOOD

A good dog deserves a home.
A good dog deserves a bone.

AMERICAN PROVERB

PURINA®

NEW

BONZ
BRAND

A 100% Nutritionally Complete Steak-Bone Shaped Dog Snack

For SMALL Dogs

ACTUAL SIZE

NET WEIGHT 27 OZ.

He don't care what you call him
as long as you call him to supper.

COWBOY ADAGE

I went to an exclusive kennel club. . . . There was a
sign out front: "No Dogs Allowed."

PHIL FOSTER
COMEDIAN

DOG CLUB®

MEAT FLAVOR

COMPLETE FOR NORMAL MAINTENANCE OF ADULT DOGS

DOG FOOD

NET WT 15 OZ · 425 GRAMS

DOG HOUSE
Food Products Company of America
Chicago, Illinois

No home is complete without the patter of doggie feet.

DOG OWNER'S ADAGE

Love is the emotion that a woman feels always for a
poodle dog and sometimes for a man.

GEORGE JEAN NATHAN

DRAMA CRITIC

French's
doggie donuts

Happiness to a dog is what lies
on the other side of a fence.

DOG OWNER'S ADAGE

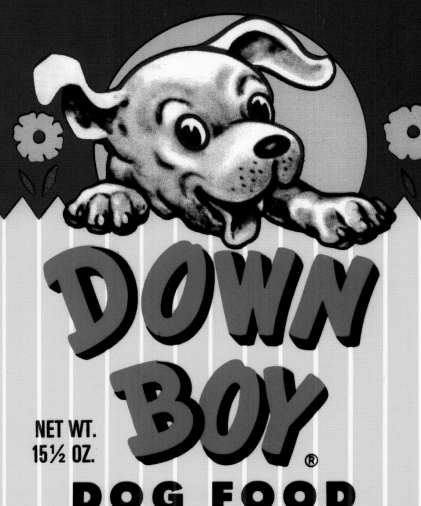

NET WT.
15½ OZ.

DOWN BOY®

DOG FOOD

Some dog I got too. We call him Egypt.
Because in every room he leaves a pyramid.

RODNEY DANGERFIELD
COMEDIAN

A well-trained dog will make no attempt
to share your lunch. He will just make you
feel so guilty that you cannot enjoy it.

HELEN THOMSON
WRITER

Fetch
DOG FOOD
NET WEIGHT
2 lbs.
ANOTHER FINE
MILK-BONE
BRAND
PRODUCT

FIDO
J-K-B Distributing Company
Los Angeles, California

I wonder if other dogs think poodles
are members of a weird religious cult.

RITA RUDNER

COMEDIAN

FIDO

DOG & CAT FOOD

NET WT. 15 OZ.

My goal in life is to be as awesome
as my dog thinks I am.

ANON.

ACME

Fiesta

A Feast for Your Pet

BEEF
& BEEF BY-PRODUCTS

DOG FOOD

FLAG
Flag Packing Company
Brooklyn, New York

The truth is out there somewhere,
but the dog needs to be walked.

D. T. MAX
WRITER

Flag

dog food

CONTENTS 15½ OZ.

FRISKIES
Carnation Company
Los Angeles, California

If you live with dogs, you'll never
run out of things to write about.

SHARON DELAROSE

WRITER

Friskies ®

LIVER
FLAVOR

DOG FOOD

A Carnation PRODUCT ®

FULMEAL
Plus Poultry
Siloam Springs, Arkansas

Life is a series of dogs.

GEORGE CARLIN
COMEDIAN

FulMeal

BRAND

Chicken Flavored

DOG FOOD

✳ *Cats like it too!*

I spilled spot remover on my dog.
Now he's gone.

STEVEN WRIGHT
COMEDIAN

Never trust a dog to watch your food.

AMERICAN PROVERB

COMPLETELY NEW FORM

GRO·PUP
BAR·B·CHEW
DOG FOOD

If you think dogs can't count,
try putting three dog biscuits in your pocket
and then giving Fido only two of them.

PHIL PASTORET

COLUMNIST

You can talk to a dog all day long, but he's just looking at you and thinking, "Where's the ball?"

MIKE MYERS

COMEDIAN

HI-VITA
Hi-Vita Pet Food Company
Huntington Park, California

There is much to learn from the dog.
For example, if you stare at someone long enough,
eventually you'll get what you want.

AUTHOR

HI-VITA DOG FOOD

CATS TOO!

NET WEIGHT 15 OZ.

HURRY
Allan Distributing Company
Sacramento, California

When your children are teenagers,
it's important to have a dog so someone
in the house is happy to see you.

NORA EPHRON
WRITER

Hurry

BRAND

DOG & CAT FOOD

NET WEIGHT 15 OZ.

If your dog is fat, you aren't getting enough exercise.

AMERICAN PROVERB

CHICKEN FLAVOR

COMPLETE AND BALANCED

HUSH PUP

DOG FOOD

NET WT. 15½ OZ.   439 GMS.

HUSKY
Hygrade Packers Company
Vancouver, Canada

Everyone on the premises is a vegetarian,
except the dog.

FRONT DOOR SIGN

Husky

BRAND

DOG FOOD

Fortified with Liver

IDEAL
Wilson & Company
Chicago, Illinois

The ideal dog food would be a ration
that tastes like mailman.

ANON.

When people see a dachshund,
they have to yell, "A wiener dog!"
Like "A rainbow!" "A shooting star!"
"A clown!"

KEVIN KLING
WRITER

JEZ

Ground

BEEF & BEEF BY-PRODUCTS

DOG FOOD

NET WT. 14 OZ.

JOY BOY
Custom Pet Food Packers
Princess Anne, Maryland

Animals may be our friends.
But they won't pick you up at the airport.

BOBCAT GOLDTHWAITH

COMEDIAN

Some of my best leading men
have been dogs and horses.

ELIZABETH TAYLOR

ACTRESS

KASCO
Kasco Complete Dog Ration
Waverly, New York

Happiness is dog-shaped, I say.

CHAPMAN PINCHER

WRITER

New!

KASCO®

EXPANDED
DOG FOOD

IN
DELICIOUS
BITE-SIZE
Morsels

I should be so lucky to have my dog's life!

ANONYMOUS NINE-TO-FIVER

He was the sweetest creature I ever saw.
He's the only dog I ever saw kiss a cat.

CHARLES KRAUTHAMMER
COLUMNIST

If you want the best seat in the house . . . move the dog.

DOG OWNER'S ADAGE

Peddy

DOG FOOD
(GOOD FOR CATS TOO)

NET
WT.
15 OZ.

No matter how little money and how few possessions
you own, having a dog makes you rich.

LOUIS SABIN

WRITER

PENNY
DOG FOOD
NET WT. 15½ OZ.

Cats Too!

French's
people

NET WT. 6 1/2 OZ. (185 g)

crackers
for dogs

THE PEOPLE DOGS LOVE TO EAT!

PLEASE
Pet Food Company
Portland, Oregon

When you feel lousy, puppy therapy is indicated.

SARA PARETSKY

WRITER

Please
DOG FOOD
NET WEIGHT 15 OZ.

POOCH
Safeway Stores
Oakland, California

His ears were often the first thing to catch my tears.

ELIZABETH BARRETT BROWNING

POET

Pooch

CHICKEN FLAVOR
DOG FOOD
NET WT. 15 1/2 OZ. METRIC EQUIV. 439g

POOCH PUNCH
Colgate Palmolive Company
New York, New York

My wife kisses the dog on the lips,
yet she won't drink from my glass.

RODNEY DANGERFIELD
COMEDIAN

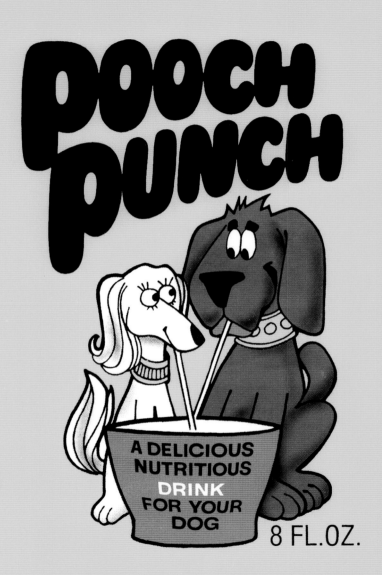

PURINA DOG CHOW
Ralston Purina Company
St. Louis, Missouri

Dog lovers are a good breed themselves.

GLADYS TABER

WRITER

POMERIAN   CHIHUAHUA   BEAGLE

Flavor so rich, nutrition so complete . . .
ALL YOU ADD IS LOVE

PURINA
DOG CHOW

THE **EAGER EATER** DOG FOOD

NET WT. 10 LBS

RAGS
Bush Bros. & Company
Clinton, Tennessee

No one appreciates the very special genius
of your conversation as the dog does.

CHRISTOPHER MORLEY

WRITER

FOR CATS AND PUPPIES TOO!

RED HEART
John Morrell & Company
Chicago, Illinois

Dogs never lie about love.

JEFFREY MASSON
WRITER

Morrell

RED HEART

DOG FOOD

FISH FLAVOR

NET WT. 15½ OZ.

RINGO
Font E Hijos Corporation
San Juan, Puerto Rico

The reason I love my dog so much is because
when I come home, he's the only one in the
world who treats me like I'm the Beatles.

BILL MAHER

HUMORIST

RINGO

DOG FOOD

NET WT. 15½ OZ.

Ever wonder where you'd end up if you took
your dog for a walk and never once
pulled back on the leash?

ROBERT BRAULT

WRITER

Romp

IT'S NEW!

DOG FOOD

WITH VITAMINS A AND D2

SPECIAL DIET FOR
WARM CLIMATE DOGS

ROSCO
National Pet Food Corporation
Long Beach, California

My sunshine doesn't come from the skies,
it comes from the love in my dog's eyes.

ANON.

ROSCO.

DOG FOOD

NET WT 15 OZ

ROVER
Rover Strongheart Company
Vancouver, Canada

The journey of life is sweeter when traveled with a dog.

DOG LOVER'S ADAGE

ROVER BRAND

DOG FOOD

LEAN RED MEAT WITH LIVER

Never underestimate the warmth of a wet nose.

DOG LOVER'S ADAGE

SPORT
Bush Bros. & Company
Cinton, Tennessee

If it wasn't for dogs, some people
would never go for a walk.

AMERICAN PROVERB

SUM
L.H. Chessher & Company
Nixon, Texas

All knowledge, the totality of all questions and all
answers, is contained in the dog.

FRANZ KAFKA
WRITER

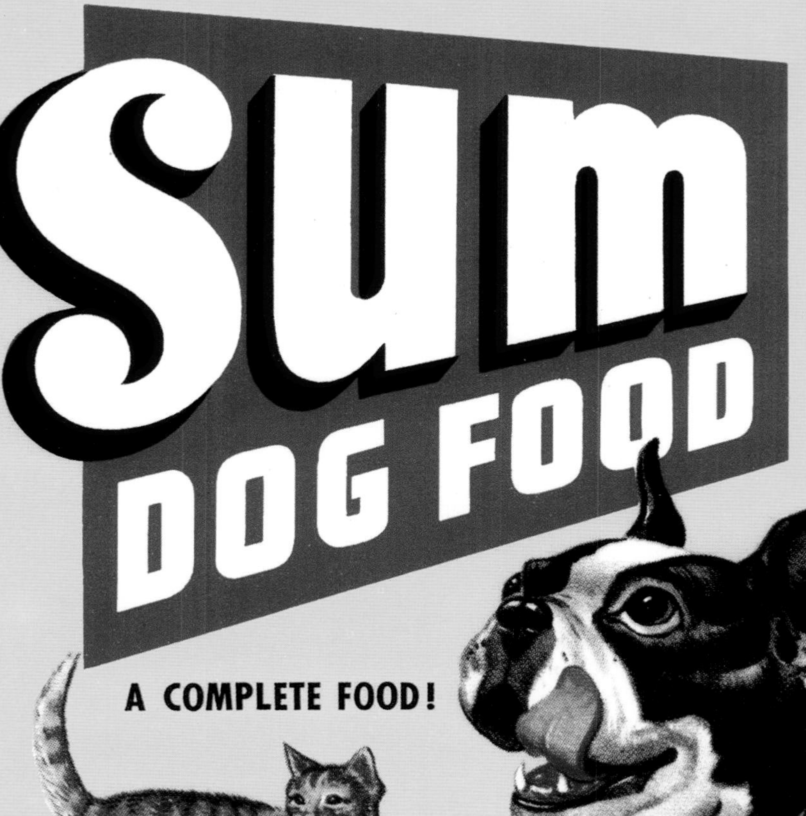

SUM
DOG FOOD
A COMPLETE FOOD!
CATS WANT SUM TOO!

THOROBRED
The Thorobred Company
Waynesville, Ohio

Go where your nose leads you.

AMERICAN PROVERB

NEW!

Thorobred ®

INSTANT MEAL
DOG FOOD

THE THOROBRED CO.

NEW!

My dog winks at me sometimes. I always wink back
in case it's some sort of code.

ANONYMOUS CANINE CONSPIRACY THEORIST

TONI
A & R Pet Food
Buffalo, New York

A dog desires affection more than dinner. Well, almost.

CHARLOTTE GRAY

WRITER

If you get to thinkin' you're a person of some influence,
try orderin' somebody else's dog around.

COWBOY ADAGE

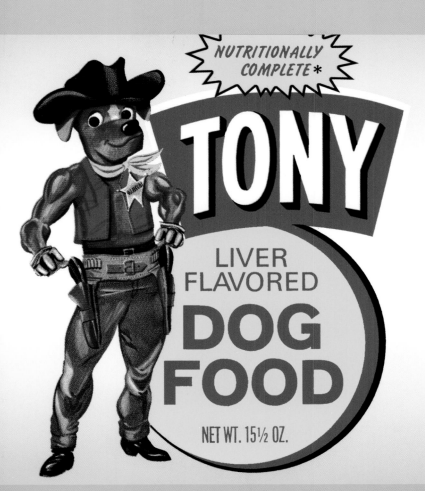

TOP DOG
Western Family Foods
San Francisco, California

The biggest dog has been a pup.

JOAQUIN MILLER

POET

DOG FOOD

NET WT. 15½ OZ.

WAYNE
Wayne Allied Mills
Fort Wayne, Indiana

In times of joy, all of us wished we possessed
a tail we could wag.

W. H. AUDEN

POET

WAYNE
DOG FOOD

It's a real
TAIL WAGGER®

™

WOW!
Acme Packers
Thomasville, Georgia

You had me at bow wow.

JACK ZIEGLER

CARTOONIST

"88"
"88" Super Markets
Stockton, California

Dogs never bite me. Just humans.

MARILYN MONROE

ACTRESS

Why, that dog is practically a Phi Beta Kappa.
She can sit up and beg, and she can give her paw—
I don't say she will, but she can.

DOROTHY PARKER

WRITER

Dexter Duke:

SIMMONDS

100%

A PROTEIN FOOD FOR PETS

TRADE MARK

Dog Food: A Brief History

Ever consider what [pets] must think of us? I mean, here we come back
from a grocery store with the most amazing haul—chicken, pork, half a cow.
They must think we're the greatest hunters on earth!

ANNE TYLER
WRITER

Sometimes we spoil our pets, so it's no surprise that throughout history the very wealthy have prepared cuisine for their canines that would have been the envy of even well-off commoners. In the 1800s, for example, Cixi, the Empress of China, fed her palace dogs such delicacies as shark fin, quail breast, and antelope milk. In eighteenth-century Europe, noblemen fed their regal hunting dogs repasts of roast duck and cake, and sated their thirst with liquors. Dogs in less aristocratic households, however, had meager diets and were fed only what their owners could spare——crusts of bread, scraps of meat, bare bones, fallen pieces of potato, discarded bits of cabbage, and whatever else they could scrounge on their own. But regardless of "social status"— whether princely thoroughbred or pauper pooch——there was no cuisine created specifically for dogs.

The Victorian era saw a rise in urban households where leisure time was increasingly common and pets were regarded as "luxury items." As a result, pet food was more closely considered. Home-prepared dog food might have consisted of ox trotters, vegetables, and oatmeal, all boiled into a stew. Around the same time, sea biscuits, the centuries-old sailor's fare of vitamin-enriched, nonperishable, hardened dough, was found to be a favorite treat for shipyard pups and strays. This seaman's food was repurposed into, and heavily marketed as, the classic boned-shaped dog biscuit we know today and quickly became the first commercial dog food. Sold in bulk, dog biscuits made of wheat, vegetables, beetroot, and beef gravy became a common item on the weekly grocery list.

Pet food manufacturing was a fully fledged industry by the turn of the twentieth century, and by the early 1940s, moist meat-based canned dog food had a significant share of the market. However, a shortage of tin during World War II meant no more canned foods for dogs or their owners, at least for a while. Luckily, technology for food preservation was prescient, and companies had already started experimenting with dry dog food, producing it in much the same way as popular crunchy cereals. The process involved taking a combination of ingredients—meat, grains, and vegetables—grinding and cooking them together, and extruding the mixture through a tube while puffing it with air to create little bite-sized shapes. Afterward the food was baked and coated with flavors and nutrients—much the same as the kibble we are familiar with today.

The decades that followed saw a return of the tin can, and more and more dog foods started hitting grocery and pet store shelves with varieties of liver, beef, and chicken flavors. Dogs and their owners were once again spoiled, this time by the plurality of choices offered. By the 1970s there were hundreds of pet foods on the market, each vying for the attention of dog owners looking to treat their pooches to something special. In addition to creating a legacy of well-fed pups, each brand left behind a unique visual imprint, making for scores of labels just waiting for the right collector of cultural ephemera to pick them up for more than the tasty morsels they advertised. Luckily, someone had the foresight to snag the best and save them for posterity.

Food for thought is no substitute for the real thing.

WALT KELLY
CARTOONIST

TRIM
B.A. Bernard & Company
Philadelphia, Pennsylvania

ACKNOWLEDGMENTS
Robert Booth, Warren Debenham, Vic Fischer, Dan Goodsell, Lyn Hejinian, Marisa Samuels, and Dennis Weiss. Dedicated to Corky and Rover.

INGREDIENTS
Beef, Cracked Wheat, Wheat Bran, Soybean Meal, Carrots, Cod Liver Oil, Salt, Onion Powder, Garlic Powder, Water Sufficient for Processing.

ANALYSIS

Neil Berliner.....humor consultant	Crude Protein, not less than.....13%
Peter Beren................book agent	Crude Fiber, not less than..........4%
Dustin Jones......................editor	Crude Fat, not more than...........1%
	Moisture, not more than...........74%

DISCLAIMER
Best efforts were made to ensure the accuracy of the attributions of selected quotes. Notification to the publisher of any inaccuracies will result in an amendment in future editions.

PACKED BY
Warren Dotz
Masud Husain

COOKED IN
THE CAN

VACUUM
PACKED

KEEP YOUR DOG   IN TRIM

Trim

DOG FOOD

Warren Dotz is a collector of pop culture ephemera and author of eleven books on advertising, design, and commercial label art. His commentary has appeared in *Advertising Age, Adweek,* and the *New York Times Magazine.* He lives and works in San Francisco and New York City.

Masud Husain is a graphic designer, branding specialist, and avid collector of American advertising ephemera. He designed and co-authored the award-winning books *Meet Mr. Product* and *Ad Boy* with Warren Dotz. He lives and works in Albany, California.